Gold~Dust and Calm

A collection of watercolours by Robert Evans Creer

text by Valerie Cottle

Published: 2007
ISBN: 9780955404337
Copyright: *Manx Heritage Foundation*
Published by the Manx Heritage Foundation, PO Box 1986, Douglas, Isle of Man.
www.manxheritage.org

*'What a boom of sunshine! It is
quite glorious. The air is full
of gold-dust and calm…'*

The Manx National Poet, the Revd T.E. Brown,
in a letter written from Ramsey to his niece
Nelly Brown, 28th September 1895.

Introduction

ROBERT EVANS CREER was born in Ramsey in 1838, the eldest son of William Creer, corn merchant, baker and harbourmaster, and his wife Esther (*née* Sayle). He was educated in Ramsey, and worked as a clerk at Corkill's the drapers until his marriage in 1865 to Catharine Margaret Teare; J.J. Corkill then gave him a reference, as a result of which he obtained a job with the Mersey Docks & Harbour Board. The young couple moved to Bootle, and Robert worked for the MDHB from 1866 until 1875, then as a manager with Blackledge's Bakery in Liverpool until he retired at the age of seventy-five. He and Catharine had thirteen children, not all of whom survived infancy.

Robert returned to the Isle of Man as often as his family and business commitments allowed, and after his mother's death in 1875 embarked on the hobby of sketching and painting which would occupy much of his spare time for the rest of his life. He painted some English, Scottish and Welsh scenery, but ninety of his 147 surviving watercolours are of the Isle of Man.

It was his habit to make sketches during his visits to the Island, usually working them up into finished paintings within a few months of his return to Liverpool. According to family tradition, he painted after his wife and children had gone to bed, and often into the small hours of the morning. Since he always stayed with family members in Ramsey, the majority of his paintings are of the north of the Island. The Creers had an extensive collection of relatives, many of them farming in the north and west, and the paintings are often of landscapes with family connections – Balladha at Dalby, farmed by Quirk cousins, Berrag at St Judes, farmed by the Corletts, and other relatives' properties in Jurby, Bride, Maughold and Lezayre. In an evocative inscription on the back of an 1881 painting (page 23), Robert noted that in a boat on the dub at Berrag 'John Corlett and I spent many, many happy hours in our

Robert Evans Creer (1838-1915).

young days. Nearly every inch of land and water represented is reminiscent to me of some adventure'.

He was very much the amateur, although a few of his paintings show felicitous techniques – the sea in the last painting in the collection, dated 1911 (page 49) is especially well handled. His work varies very much in its standards and could generally be described as naive. He is no Archibald Knox, who could 'paint the wind'; he is uncertain in his handling of shadows, and seldom indicates where his light is coming from or shows any movement in his foliage or clouds. There is no evidence that he was anything but self-taught, although an inscription on the back of one picture (page 57) records an excursion from Port St Mary with the better-known Manx artist Flaxney Stowell. He also mentions a Mr Gillard in Liverpool, although it has not been possible to trace an art teacher of that name.

Although Creer makes no such claim, a moonlit scene of the jagged rocks at Scarlett (page 54) is reminiscent of the great German Romantic painter Caspar David Friedrich (1774-1840), and it is interesting to surmise what paintings of quality he may have seen. During his artistic career (1875-1914) the city of Liverpool offered enthusiasts many opportunities to see art of the highest quality. The Walker Art Gallery

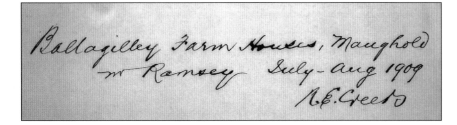

Almost all Creer's watercolours have a handwritten inscription on the back detailing where and when they were sketched and painted.

A self-portrait in profile, probably in his late 30s.

was opened in 1877, attracting 324,117 visitors in its first four months; it is tempting to think that Robert might have been amongst them. Between 1871 and 1910 the city council bought some 150 works from the annual autumn exhibitions held at the William Brown Library and Museum, the first systematic attempt by any British public body to make a collection of contemporary works available to the general public.

But for anyone interested in the Isle of Man the value of Creer's work lies not in any artistic merit, but in his portrayal of rural Manx life in the closing decades of the nineteenth century. His painting years saw the Island opened up in an unprecedented way through the burgeoning visiting industry. By the 1870s Douglas was building extensive new facilities; by the summer season of 1887 347,968 visitors arrived in the Island between May and September, and they certainly did not all stay in the capital. The first steam railway line was opened between Douglas and Peel in 1873, followed by the Douglas-Port Erin route a year later and a line from St Johns to Ramsey in 1879. In Ramsey the construction of the Queen's Pier in 1886 meant that steamers could bring passengers to the town at all states of the tide. The Mooragh Park was opened in 1887. During the 1890s the construction of the Manx Electric Railway on the 'scenic route' between Douglas and Ramsey made the northern town even more popular, and its resident population rose from 2,891 in 1861 to 4,866 in 1891.

But Robert Evans Creer depicted little or none of this. He concentrated on timeless rural and coastal scenes in the remoter parts of the Island. Some of his landscapes show buildings which are instantly recognisable: the Albert Tower above Ramsey, the Langness and Calf of Man lighthouses, grand houses such as Crogga at Santon and Balladoole, Arbory, the church at Bride and chapels at Cardle and Tholt-y-Will. The smaller buildings he depicts are half hidden in verdant foliage, his horses

An autumnal view in Glen Auldyn (1881).

and cattle graze in peaceful green pastures, his boats sail on calm seas – almost as a child might paint them. The farmhouse he painted at Berrag (page 22) has today lost its old garden wall and is considerably extended and sparkling with new paint, but the Poylly Dub where Robert and his cousin John Corlett junior played in their boat is still there. Other scenes are of quiet country lanes, streams and hills where little has changed in more than a century since he made his first sketches.

Particularly interesting is Creer's treatment of the often-solitary human figures which inhabit his landscapes. They appear at first to be rather wooden, insignificant little people placed into the scenery as an afterthought, but they repay closer study. We know who some of them are. John Corlett junior stands sturdily outside Berrag; the young woman who perches uneasily in her best white muslin on a gate at the back of Claughbane House is thought to be one of his two nieces, Frances or Edith Cleator. Others are not identified: a well-dressed couple stand, slightly apart, against a background of immaculate lawns and a gardener rolling a gravel path at Glen Wyllin; two black-clad women with elaborate hats are almost hidden above the weir at Sulby Glen; a young woman with a parasol talks to a boy in knickerbockers on Ramsey beach; two young people lounging on the beach at Balladha, south of Niarbyl, could be visitors to the Island but are likely to be more cousins, from the Quirk family who farmed there.

Where there are two or more people in Creer's pictures they are often standing rather uneasily apart, or heading away from each other. A notable exception is the explicitly titled 'Twilight Spooning, 9pm' of 1908, in which a happily entwined couple make their way in the gloaming along a country road (page 42). A more enigmatic pair of figures appear in an 1886 view of the road near Ballaghennie, Bride (page 27). A horse and sheep graze on slopes to the left, and sunrays stream down from a dark cloud in the background. But what is

On the road near Rhenwee, Andreas.

'Ballamanaugh House, Sulby Claddagh. Primrose Hill behind. April 1905'. Creer uses the English version of the name for the hill which is now universally known as Cronk Sumark.

happening here? A woman in a bonnet and carrying a reticule is walking down the road towards us. Fifty yards away a man is standing, his body in profile. Is he merely looking at the sheep in the field, or is he looking down the road towards the retreating woman? Are they acquaintances who have just finished a conversation, or could they be lovers who have quarrelled? It is quite mystifying to take a magnifying glass to this picture and discover that the man has in fact no face at all; as so often with his very small figures, Creer has simply painted the man in over the landscape, and between his hat and his clothed body there is nothing but the green hedge behind him.

So widely spread, geographically speaking, are the subjects of Creer's Manx paintings – from the lighthouse at the Point of Ayre to the Calf and the Chicken Rock – that it is interesting to surmise how he must have got around. He could almost certainly have had the loan of a bone-shaker bicycle from someone in Ramsey. After 1879 he could have used the steam railway from Ramsey to St Johns, which linked up with the other lines to Peel, Douglas and the south, and by the 1890s he could have travelled on the electric tram down past Maughold and Laxey. Horse-drawn coaches had been operated from Ramsey from the early years of the century. The best-known coach owner was James Crowe, mentioned in several of T.E. Brown's humorous poems, whose business was continued into the 1880s, and there were at least half a dozen different 'car proprietors' advertising their services in Ramsey in the 1890s.

Robert Evans Creer's pastimes were not limited to painting. A staunch Methodist, he contributed biographical notes on 'Some Old Liverpool Wesleyans' to *The Wesleyan*, and was a prolific composer of hymns; the Manx National Heritage library holds a 288-page manuscript book of his compositions. He took delight in the compilation of family trees detailing his numerous relations, with

On the Baldhoon road above Laxey, with Cairn
Gerjoil in the distance, 1903 (detail).

historical notes and such intriguing details as – of one Mira Margaret Radcliffe – 'Authoress of Ina and Other Poems; Mira was jilted by a Liverpool merchant in early life and was queer ever after'. He also left to his family a series of 'pen portraits' of relatives and friends. A particularly pleasing one is his account of the Corletts of Berrag. Mr Corlett was 'our nearest and dearest relation and friend'; 'If we had a holiday word was sent to Berrag, and a conveyance was gladly sent for us, & brought us back. We might go there when we pleased, stay as long as we liked, & had always the heartiest welcome. In 1861, being in ill health I spent three or four months there, & the dear old gentleman shed tears that we had to part...'

After Creer's death in 1915 his watercolours passed to his son, Robert Evans Creer junior, then via Frank Herbert Creer to a grandson, Raymond Frank Creer, who having no children left the Manx paintings on his death in 2001 to Manx National Heritage. They had by then survived two World Wars and a number of house moves, but had been carefully cared for by Raymond and his wife Beryl. They were temporarily mislaid after Raymond's death, but a few years later were discovered wrapped in acid-free tissue paper in home-made folders in a linen cupboard. A great-granddaughter, Kate Keown, and her husband John handed the collection over to Manx National Heritage in 2006.

We have no precise evidence that Robert Evans Creer met the Revd T.E. Brown, who lived in retirement in Ramsey for four years until his death in 1897, but it would be surprising if the paths of the Manx National Poet and such a frequent visitor, with so many relatives in Ramsey, had not crossed. Both dearly loved the peace and beauty of the Manx countryside – and both, indeed, were long exiled from it. So it seemed appropriate to use some of Brown's words as a title for this book...

This painting, with its pleasing contrast between a neat garden in north Ramsey and the wild slopes of Sky Hill beyond, is a view from The Cottage in what was then called Sandy Road. This, also known as Victoria Cottage and subsequently as Cronk Ghennie, belonged to the Creer family. It still stands – although under threat of demolition – at the junction of the Jurby and Andreas Roads. The painting is undated, but shows the view towards the house opposite, which still has finials on its slate roof. The Jurby Road runs between the double set of Ballacorey brick and stone walls.

Captioned 'Behind Claughbane House, Ramsey, 1897', the perilously perched young woman in this painting is believed by Robert Evans Creer's descendants to be one of his Cleator nieces, either Frances or Edith. His sister Esther had married a grocer, Robert Cleator, and given birth to the two girls, but died while they were still very young; they were brought up by their maternal grandmother. Edith later married the Ramsey photographer G. B. Cowen, but she too died following childbirth, aged only twenty-nine, so it is more likely that this is her sister Frances.

Creer did not caption this picture, but it is clearly of Ballure Church, with houses overlooking the south beach (or 'ladies' bathing shore') and Maughold headlands in the background. With the parish church at Maughold being at such a distance, Ballure was built as a chapel of ease in the seventeenth century, and served the citizens of Ramsey until the consecration of the more conveniently-sited St Paul's in 1822. It several times fell into a ruinous state, being restored in 1706, 1746 and again more thoroughly in 1851. It has now been deconsecrated and converted into a private house.

Ramsey's Mooragh Park. Although the painting itself bears the date 1881, Creer's inscription on the back says June 1891. This must be correct, as in 1881 the Commissioners had only just bought a tidal swamp on the site with a view to creating the park, which was opened in 1887. The passing steamship is almost certainly the Isle of Man Steam Packet's *Tynwald* (3), launched in 1891, which often ran from Douglas to Whitehaven via Ramsey. It subsequently became the eccentric millionaire Colby Cubbin's private yacht *Western Isles*, was requisitioned by the Admiralty during World War II, and finally scuttled in 1951.

Maughold Head from the Mooragh, dated 'about 1890'. A young woman with a parasol talks to a boy in knickerbockers, with a racing skiff and Manx 'nickies' or luggers on the bay behind them. The wide sweep of Ramsey sands had for some years been extolled as one of the town's attractions. To the right can be seen the 2,248ft. Queen's Pier, which for the first time enabled low water landings. Designed by Sir John Goode and opened by Bishop Rowley Hill in 1886, it had a railway line laid along it and was illuminated by gaslight. It would be further extended in 1894 and by 1906 was used by a record 36,000 passengers.

R.E.Creer 1888

Creer captioned this delightfully naive little study 'Calm – Ramsey Bay – off pier. April 1888'. Another hand, believed to be that of a granddaughter, Emma Catharine Creer, has added a doggerel verse on the back, 'Fred and Archie in the boat / Trying hard to keep afloat / Fred is asking Archie what'll / Be inside the floating bottle?' A passing steam yacht adds interest to the scene; it is difficult to gauge its scale, but it could be one of the smaller private vessels popular amongst the wealthy at this period. 'Fred and Archie' are obviously becalmed, but it does not seem to be attracting their interest.

Ramsey South Pier at low tide, painted in 1881. According to Constance Radcliffe in *Shining By the Sea*, the first pier or quay in Ramsey, corresponding to the first wide section of the present South Pier, was probably built in the 1740s. In 1771 the Harbour Minutes recorded that 'The Pier on the South side of the River where vessels usually moor is in good repair and condition. The Lighthouse has been lately glazed and repaired'. The North Pier was constructed in 1829 to stop sand and gravel collecting on the north side of the South Pier, where vessels moored, but it would appear from this picture that it could still be a problem.

A view (undated) of the Albert Tower from Claughbane, where there is still a curving track like this in the plantation. The tower was built in 1849 and bears the inscription, 'ALBERT TOWER. Erected on the spot where H.R.H. Prince Albert stood to view Ramsey and its neighbourhood during the visit of Her Most Gracious Majesty Queen Victoria to Ramsey Bay, the XXth September. MDCCCCLVII'. The Queen, being unwell, stayed on board the Royal Yacht, but the Prince 'could not restrain his expressions of gratification and delight' when he ascended the hill. The vessel, probably heading for the Queen's Pier, is likely to be either the *King Orry*(2) or *Snaefell*(2).

'Between the Beardhown & the Grove, near Ramsey. April 1889'. This should more correctly be Bayr Dhowin, the Deep Road, which runs from the Jurby Road steeply down to the Whitebridge across the Sulby River. The point which most closely resembles this scene is in fact in the modern Richmond Road, very close to the Grove. The farmer's wife (stylishly wearing a high-crowned hat which perhaps is her husband's) seems quite happy to allow her cattle to graze freely on the grass verges, thick with wild flowers. The stiffcart is of the most basic kind, with boards running from front to back and an open back to facilitate easy loading.

Robert Evans Creer captioned this painting 'From Point of Ayre lighthouse (top)', and the terrain nearest his viewpoint, with its dense mounds of gorse and heather, is certainly typical of the Ayres. Mate's *The Isle of Man Illustrated* of 1902 described the 'noble lighthouse and fog-signal station... [where] steamers pass within a cable length of the shore, and the beach slopes into deep water with alarming steepness'. The 99ft. lighthouse, designed by Robert Stevenson and first lit in 1818, was certainly a good vantage point but, as he often did, Creer seems considerably to have foreshortened his view towards the south and Maughold Head.

The Lhen Trench (undated). It is likely that this scene is near the Lhen end of the Trench, where there are still signs on either side of it of old 'lazy beds', raised by hand to create an adequate depth of soil for potatoes and other crops. These low, parallel banks were often fertilised with manure or seaweed. The Lhen Trench (or River) also links up to the south with the Killane River, and is part of the drainage system from the large lake which in mediaeval times still occupied the Curragh area. In *The Naturalist in the Isle of Man* (1972) Larch Garrad described both the Lhen and Killane Rivers as 'largely artificial creations'.

Creer's cousin John Corlett junior is depicted in 1880, standing sturdily outside his family home at Berrag, Jurby. The Corletts of Berrag were related to Creer through both his parents, and the families were the closest of friends; as children Robert and his brother and sister stayed at Berrag as often as they could think up a reason to do so, always receiving a warm welcome, and the young Corletts would in return come to stay with them in Ramsey. John Corlett senior was the main benefactor of Sandygate Methodist Chapel. Creer recorded sadly that after their parents' deaths John Corlett junior and his brother Robert took to drink and died in early middle age.

'The Pohlly dub, Berrag, Jurby, 1881, in a boat on which John Corlett and I spent many, many happy hours in our young days. Nearly every inch of land and water represented is reminiscent to me of some adventure'. Creer frequently reminisced about the happy times he and his brother and sister had enjoyed with the Corlett family. The house at Berrag has now been modernised and extended, but still has a particularly impressive range of original outbuildings. This large dub remains behind it, but is now thickly planted with trees on the far bank so that the landscape to the north is no longer visible.

'In front of Berrag house, 1876/8'. One of the advantages enjoyed by people who live on the Island's northern plain is the wonderful view of the hills they have as they look southwards. Here Snaefell looms over the entrance to Sulby Glen, and the outline of the volcanic plug of Cronk Sumark can be seen clearly to the left, below the peak of Slieu Managh. Cultivated fields stretch far further up the hillsides than they do today. A close examination of the centre of this picture reveals a steam train puffing its way across the fields from right to left, en route from St Johns via Ballaugh to Ramsey.

'St Bridget's Church, Bride' was sketched on 15th July 1886 and painted little more than a week later. The building was at that time only about fourteen years old; its foundation stone was laid in 1869 and the first service was held in 1872, but it was not actually consecrated until 1876. It was designed by the architect Joseph Henry Christian, London-born but of Manx descent. It replaced an ancient treen church, very much along the lines of the parish church at Malew, which had dated from around 1200. The original church on the site was supposed to have been founded by St Bride in the sixth century.

This view of 'Quayle's house near Ballaghenny, Bride' was sketched on 15th July 1886, the same day as Creer sketched Bride Church. The cottages are probably on the way towards the site of the present-day Ayres Visitor Centre, but it has not been possible to identify the site exactly. The fact that the chimney of the one in the middle is two-thirds of the way along the roof indicates an extension; the chimney would originally have been on the gable end. The young man standing on the road holds what could be a fishing rod over his shoulder, and wears trousers and a waistcoat which look as if they are made of Loaghtyn tweed.

Another painting 'On the road near Ballaghenny, Bride, October 1886'. Positively beatific beams of sunshine stream down onto the far landscape from behind a dark cloud, with the range of the Ballaghennie farm buildings to the left. It is impossible to tell whether the couple Creer depicts have enjoyed a friendly chat, or parted after having words, or whether they are complete strangers to each other. Is the man looking down the road after the woman, or is he is simply admiring the sheep in the fields? There is something mysterious about the whole scene, which might form the basis of an intriguing short story.

This view of Andreas Church and the farmstead of Ballavoddan was sketched from Rhenwee on the Regaby-Crosh Beg road on 20th July 1887 and painted during August. The church was built in 1802 using stone quarried in Sulby Glen. At the time Creer painted this view the church was notable for its 120ft bell tower, which had been added to the building, unusually linked to it only by an arch, in 1869. Today the tower can scarcely be seen above the roof from this point. Its height was reduced during World War II because it was judged a hazard to the nearby airfield; money was later supplied, but it was never rebuilt.

'Kneale's mill pond and buildings & Sky Hill, Glen Auldyn. Feb. 1886'. The trees are in full leaf, so Creer must have made his preliminary sketch in the summer of 1885. During the twentieth century the mill and its pond were incorporated as decorative features into the grounds of Milntown house, which for 600 years had been the home of the powerful Christian family. The Revd William Bell Christian died insolvent and the house and its contents were sold at public auction in 1886. His widow ran a school there until the 1920s, but only as a tenant. John Southward Kneale was the tenant miller in the 1880s.

Creer sketched this view from Lezayre Churchyard in August 1888, and made a preliminary painting that December. However he returned to it in 1896 to show the position of the Old School House and draw attention to the graves of Capt. Robert Kneale RN and Major Ewan Kneale. He seems to have been rather proud of these connections. His inscription on the back not only lovingly details Robert Kneale's kinship with the Creers and other related families, but also boasts that 'Robert Kneale's wife (or mother) was a daughter of the O'Neills of Shane's Castle, Co. Antrim, Earls of Tyrone, Kings of Ulster and earlier Kings of Ireland'!

'Cooilbane Cottage, Lezayre 1881'. The site of this dwelling behind its long, low, whitewashed walls is still immediately recognisable today, although the 'cottage' has been greatly enlarged and now boasts four reception rooms, oil-fired central heating and parking space for five cars. Estate agents have advertised it as being built *circa* 1600. One thing Robert Evans Creer could never have envisaged is that it stands now on one of the faster straights of the TT course; his cow would have been an instant casualty, although the woman making her way slowly towards the quiet Ballacaley Lane would have had a better chance of survival...

'Mrs Craine's – on road from Cooilbane to Gob-e-Volley, Lezayre. 1902'. It is unclear whether the road Creer was referring to is the main road running west from Cooilbane towards Ballaugh, or the Ballacaley Lane, but the latter is most likely. The 1901 Census returns for Lezayre include a family of four with surnames appearing variously as Caine and Craine. The mother, sixty-eight year old Judith, who lived with her seventy-three year old husband William, a retired farmer, seems the most likely candidate for Creer's 'Mrs Craine'. Appropriately enough, their address is given in the Census as Rose Cottage.

'Southwards Weir, entrance to Sulby Glen'. Creer sketched this view in 1885, and completed the painting on 13th April 1886. The Southward family had come to the bottom of Sulby Glen to set up a woollen mill in about 1830, and by 1851 Thomas E. Southward was employing six men; by then all stages of cloth production were being carried out on the premises. The mill flourished through several changes of ownership, and was particularly noted for its flannel, dyed with imported vegetable colours such as indigo and logwood. Howarth & Penrice was the last firm to run it before it finally closed in 1956.

'On Sulby River – at Southwards Cloth Mill'. Sketched in September 1894 and painted the following August. A more tranquil view of the Sulby River, in this case before it reached the weir. Creer has taken great pains with this picture, meticulously drawing and colouring the details of foliage and flowers, and very accurately depicting the great bulk of Mount Karrin, which overshadows the lower part of Sulby Glen, and its reflection in the water. A patch of purple heather is coloured in on the flank of the hill, and what appears to be a gush of water, presumably from the mill wheel, can be seen on the right hand side.

Creer has written on the back of this peaceful, contemplative scene, 'On the old road between Sulby Village and Gob-e-Volley. Sept. 1898....... in haze in distance'. Unfortunately the missing word has been cut away from the label on the back, but it is likely to have been Carrick. It is possible by going into the Ballacaley Lane at Sulby and looking diagonally across the Ballacaley Farm fields towards the bottom of the glen, to get a view, the skyline of which precisely corresponds to this picture. The direction of the shadows would indicate that the man is resting on the gate (and perhaps smoking his pipe?) fairly early in the day.

35

The back of this picture provides very precise topographical details. Creer has written 'From above Tholt-y-Will, Sulby Glen. Sulby Glen Chapel. Berrag on flat, distant land. 25/3/09. Craigmooar above the Chapel. Karrin is the highest hill on left'. This Wesleyan Methodist Chapel had been built in 1873 – the Wesleyan cause was particularly strong in this part of the Island, and of course Creer was himself a loyal disciple. His fondness for the Corletts of Berrag was such that he could identify their farm in the far distance. Beyond that, the coast of Scotland can be seen on the horizon.

Maughold Head, sketched 20th July 1886, painted five months later. This view from the sea greatly exaggerates the height of Maughold Head. The cove beneath it, between Gob ny Skey and Gob ny Strona, is the traditional landing place of the Kerruishes of Ballafayle when they first came to the Island. The modern viewer may be puzzled by the absence of the lighthouse, but in fact it was not built until 1914. It was automated in the 1990s and its buildings, large enough to house a principal and two assistant keepers and their families, are now a private dwelling.

Creer's caption here is slightly problematic, since he has written 'Maughold Head and church, from south side of Port [Mooar], June 1899', yet there is no church in the picture. But his viewpoint is easily identified, in the field just to the sea side of the modern Booilushag development, and from there the church is not visible. One reading of the object on the slope to the left is that it is a large standing stone, but there is no sign of such a thing now, nor is it marked on any old maps. An alternative view would be that the grey rocks are just an outcrop, or a miniature quarry. Today the slope is thickly covered with gorse and bracken.

'Ballagilley farm houses, Maughold. July–Aug. 1909'. The old treen farm of Ballagilley is on the road which winds from the Hibernian up over the flank of North Barrule to the Gooseneck. It was originally named for the Gill or McGill family, but they had left it before 1511; later families associated with it included the Looneys in the seventeenth century, and the Callows and Kissacks later on. Robert Evans Creer painted the farm buildings from the north, with the lower slope of Barrule beyond. The main house has since had a double gable added, and the smaller outbuildings have been demolished.

'View in Maughold on by-road between the Hibernian & Ballabarna [sic], the "Watery Road". Sept. 1914'. It has not been possible precisely to identify Creer's viewpoint. This route is not actually a road, but a public footpath which leads east from the Laxey-Ramsey road close to the Hibernian crossroads. It is also sometimes referred to as the 'Burial Road', since coffins used to be carried this way towards Maughold Church. Further down it goes through the Ballaberna farmyard, links up with School House Lane and passes the old 'central' parish schoolhouse.

'The shoulder of North Barrule from Ballaberna, Maughold ... showing the once famous Hibernia[n] Hotel, built by Rachel Looney and carried on by her'. Mrs Looney had obviously left an indelible impression on the people of Maughold. She kept the Hibernian public house in the 1830s, and was known for her interest in antiquities; workmen she employed in 1833 found the so-called Ballaberna Hoard of coins, recorded as bearing 'the inscriptions of the Henrys and the Edwards, and ... in a good state of preservation'. Described as 'a lady of parts', Rachel Looney 'in 1842 ... emigrated to Australia in pursuit of an erring spouse'.

A touching scene, 'Twilight spooning (9 p.m.) on road between Ballaglass & the Hibernia[n], Maughold', this has to be one of the most delightful of Creer's pictures. He painted it on 29th July 1908, and despite the soft veils of grey cloud this is clearly at the height of summer. The couple, not perhaps in their first youth, are tenderly wrapped around each other as they make their way slowly along the road in the gloaming; they are clearly in no hurry to reach their destination. This is one of the very few of Creer's paintings in which the human figures play a pivotal part, rather than being added as a slightly awkward afterthought.

Creer noted on the back of this painting, which he completed in July 1912, that the cottage had been the home of the poet William Kennish, born in 1799; Kennish left the Island at twenty-two, unable to speak English, but rose to be Master Carpenter of the British fleet in the Mediterranean. The farmhouse in the trees is Cardle Voar, and in the middle is the Cardle Methodist Chapel, built in 1909. William Kennish died in New York in 1862. During the late twentieth century his cottage was extended to make a substantial modern home; the Manx Heritage Foundation placed a memorial plaque on the adjacent Corrany Bridge in 1986.

'View from the top of Snaefell, looking south, 1880'. Like so many Victorian landscape painters, Creer made his topographical views more dramatic by foreshortening the perspective and exaggerating the height and inclines of mountains and crags. Here he has brought Mullagh Ouyr well into the foreground, and made the line of hills running away above the East Baldwin valley – Beinn-y-Phott, Slieau Lhost, Slieau Ree and Slieau Ruy – far more precipitous than they really are. It is interesting to see the old peat diggings on Mullagh Ouyr, and to note the man and his sheepdog admiring the view.

'The Killane Mill near Ballatear[e], Jurby. Painted January 1906'. The origins of the Killane Mill are of great antiquity – it was mentioned in the Rent Roll of 1513. It is not known whether it was still in operation when Robert Evans Creer painted it, but today the mill pond has completely disappeared – as has the lime kiln, lost to coastal erosion – and the mill building has been converted into a private house. In Mate's *The Isle of Man Illustrated* of 1902, the Revd John Quine wrote, 'In this district may still be seen sod cottages thatched with bent, the best surviving examples of the old Manx cabin'.

'Glen Wyllin, Michael (looking across high road to Slieau Froghane mountain)'. This view, sketched on 9th August 1890 and painted in February the following year, features the most idiosyncratic of the human figures which people Creer's paintings. What a pity we do not know the identity of the bearded man with his smart silk hat and rolled umbrella, and his trim companion with her leg-of-mutton sleeves and feather bonnet. They might have been dressed ready for Sunday chapel, except that the Lord's Day is not being observed; the man in the background is hard at work rolling the already immaculate gravel of the garden path.

'Balladha farm houses and the Niarbyl Point, Dalby'. Creer made the sketch for this painting on 1st September 1893. His Quirk relatives lived at Balladha, and he was obviously at pains to portray their home, their outbuildings and the ricks in their yard – carefully tied down with suggane rope and weighted with stones – as carefully as possible. The man walking across the field to look at the cows could well be a member of the family; he, his cattle and his poultry are all painted in meticulous detail. The rocks of Niarbyl stretch out to sea beyond them, and a pleasure yacht and two luggers sail peacefully in the distance.

'Balladha Beach, Dalby. Niarbyl Rocks in distance. February 1894'. If it was indeed February, it seems odd that the well-dressed couple with their straw hats are lounging in such a carefree way on the shingle, watching a steam yacht sail by beyond the rocky outline of Niarbyl. Either it was an unusually mild day, or Creer simply added them to the painting as an afterthought. The jagged black rocks are a particular feature of this beach, more usually known as Traie Vrish. The entire Dalby area is of great interest to geologists; in a mid-nineteenth century trial a small body of antimony ore was discovered here.

In this painting, dated March 1911, 'From Mona (near Dalby) to Erin (Mountains of Mourne)', Creer demonstrated a quite remarkable facility for painting an authentically rough sea. So lively is his handing of the waves here, towards the end of his painting life, that one cannot help wondering whether he had had some tuition. The seas he painted off Ramsey in the 1880s, for instance, were mostly very flat and amateurish, although the 1886 view of Maughold Head from the sea (*page 37*) showed some feeling for the movement of choppy water. Fine sunsets over the Mournes can be enjoyed from this viewpoint.

On the back of this view of Glen Rushen from Cronk-ny-Irree Lhaa Creer has listed all the visible peaks, from Slieau Whallian on the left to North Barrule, just visible over the lower slope of South Barrule, on the right. The Isle of Man Mining Company started operations by sinking a shaft on the Beckwith Lode in Glen Rushen in 1831, but they had problems with flooding throughout the lifetime of the mine, until it finally closed in 1879. By then the main shaft had been sunk to 185 fathoms. The painting is undated; all the buildings shown are still roofed, but there are no clear signs of any activity.

'Crogga from Port Soderic[k]'. This painting, completed on 13th August 1884, shows the turreted Crogga mansion house at Santon, which would have been quite a talking point at the time since it had only been completed six years earlier. In Scottish Baronial Revival style, it was designed by the Douglas architect James Cowle as a country seat for John Quayle of the Castletown banking family, the fifth generation of his family to hold the title Clerk of the Rolls. Crogga was built by James Cooper & Sons of Castletown, and is architecturally quite unlike any other building on the Island.

This study of Cass~ny-Howin was painted in fairly slapdash style in April 1886. On the promontory to the right are the remains of a fort on high ground, with a ditch and rampart to landward, which may have dated from the Celtic Iron Age and then been re-used by the Vikings. Creer's painting shows it ploughed and sown with grain right to the edge of the cliff. The Santon River is the boundary between the parishes of Santan and Malew. In mediaeval times it was the boundary between the Lord's Lands and the lands of Rushen Abbey, and had the Norse name *Korn-á*, 'corn river', because of the number of mills on its banks.

Creer made a number of paintings of the rocks at Scarlett. This one, sketched on 8th July 1889 and painted on 25th April 1890, is captioned 'The Black Rocks, Scarlett Point, Castletown, with the Stack and Langness in the distance. From Cromwell's Seat'. Cromwell's Seat is a rocky outcrop, and the path alongside the high stone wall at Scarlett is known as Cromwell's Walk, but both commemorate a local farmer rather than the Protector. The Langness lighthouse, completed in 1880, and the early nineteenth century Herring Tower (originally built as a stone beacon) can be clearly seen on the horizon.

Another view of the 'Black Rocks' at Scarlett, this time with the note that they were sketched at 9 p.m. on 8th July 1889. It is not known whether Robert Evans Creer ever had the chance to see any pictures by the great German Romantic painter Caspar David Friedrich (1774–1840), but this moonlit scene is – apart from the absence of a brooding human figure, usually seen from the back – strongly reminiscent of his work. During Creer's painting career (1875–1914) the city of Liverpool where he lived and worked offered enthusiasts many opportunities to see art of the highest quality in public galleries.

'Bradda Head, Port Erin bay and Kentraugh house' is not dated, and the identification of the house as Kentraugh is incorrect. Nothing can be seen of Port Erin bay apart from the head and the Milner Tower (built in 1871). The large house with the verandah is not Kentraugh but Balladoole, home of the Stevenson family; the verandah has since been removed, but its pillars can still be seen on a building at Balladoole Farm. The viewpoint is from fields at the back of Knock Rushen. As a Ramsey man, Creer may be forgiven for confusing the two important southside houses.

It seems that Creer, in his caption, wrote 'Cronk-ny-Irrey Lhaa and South Barrule from near Carthure Rocks, Bay-ny-Carrickey', without knowing the name of the house which stands so prominently in the middle of this painting. It is Mount Gawne (now rather elaborately refurbished, and simply called The Mount). In 1817 a much-needed Act was passed to license the issue of banknotes, and one of the first to take advantage of it was the brewer and landowner Edward Gawne, who carried on business here and until 1837 issued banknotes carrying a view of the house.

This picture, which bears signs of having been completed in a hurry and has paint trials on the back, Creer has captioned 'Port St Mary harbour breakwater. Done on a sketching day in company with Flaxney Stowell. The boat with Old Kelly in it is the one in which I afterwards went to the Chickens Lighthouse and I embarked at the little cove at the mouth of which the boat is represented as being'. His view of the Chicken Rock (*page 60*) is dated May 1893; although the sea on the Chicken Rock painting looks reasonably calm, he was a brave man to have entrusted himself to the inscrutable Old Kelly in such a tiny boat.

All the components of this picture have been carefully labelled on the back, 'View from near Cregneash showing Bradda Point [*sic*] on left, Fleshwick valley and hill on right, Cronk-ny-Irrey Lhaa, Dalby (light greens), & Peel Hill in distance'. Creer sketched the view on 27th June 1889 and finished the painting in the August. The viewpoint would appear to have been somewhere high up in the fields between The Howe and Balnahowe farm, since only from here can a clear view be obtained right through past Fleshwick and the Carnanes to Corrin's Folly on Peel Hill.

'The Calf of Man from near Cregneash'. This view was sketched on 27th June 1889 and painted the following February. The Calf belonged to members of the Carey family (after whom one of the small landing stages on the north side was named) from 1845-1910. Col. George Carey, who built the islet's farmhouse with its well-known inscription *Parva domus, magna quies* (A small house, great peace), was living there in some style at this time with his family, several servants and a gamekeeper. A noted oarsman, he was said to have been able to row across the Sound against an eight-knot current.

Creer's 1893 view of the Chicken Rock and Calf of Man lighthouses. The two lighthouses were built on the Calf in 1818, their lights aligned to indicate the submerged hazard of the rock. A light tower was completed and brought into operation in 1875 on the Chicken Rock itself, and the lights on the Calf then fell into disuse. Since then, a new manned lighthouse was built on the Calf in 1968; this in its turn was automated in 1995, and has now been abandoned again. An upgraded Chicken Rock light began showing its new range of twenty-one nautical miles with effect from 13th June 2007.

'The Northern Mountains of the Isle of Man from St Marks – Ballavarvane trees in fore'. Creer sketched this view in August 1884 and completed the painting the following April, writing in the names of all the peaks in the lower margin, and their heights on the back. They extend from Greeba on the left round to Cronk Gerjoil on the far right.

Robert Evans Creer painted in locations around Merseyside, in the Lake District, Scotland and North Wales as well as in the Isle of Man. This study, made in 1884, is of the two great castles which stand sentinel 500ft above the Cheshire Plain, Beeston and Peckforton. Few artists could resist them. Creer shows the real mediaeval castle of Beeston (dating from 1225, and in ruins ever since the Civil War) illuminated to the right of the picture. Peckforton, a Victorian pastiche built between 1844–1851 for a local MP, and today a luxury hotel, is in the shadows on the left.

Y Tryfan has been described as 'the most remarkable rock mountain in Wales ... what it lacks in height it makes up in picturesque outline'. Ten miles west of Bettws-y-Coed, it measures only 3,010ft, but its summit forms a dramatic ridge with three separate peaks, the middle one being the highest and crowned with two large stones visible from the road. Creer did this painting in 1883, giving the black bulk of the mountain added impact by wrapping a white wisp of cloud around its summit. On the back of the painting he has written 'Tryfaen, Galtygogo 1883'. Gallt yr Ogof is a ridge south east of the mountain, between Tryfan and Capel Curig.

Acknowledgements & Bibliography

The author would like to acknowledge the assistance of Kate Keown, who supplied all the information on the life of her great-grandfather Robert Evans Creer; Fenella Bazin, Frank Cowin, Richard Danielson, Carys Howell, Elfyn Jones, Peter Kelly, Keith Kerruish, J. David Moore, Eva Wilson and (at Manx National Heritage) Erica Spencer, Andrew Johnson, Matthew Richardson and Yvonne Cresswell, for other information, advice and suggestions; and the various landowners who allowed her onto their properties to identify Robert Evans Creer's viewpoints.

Garrad, L.S., *The Naturalist in the Isle of Man*, 1972.
Haskett Smith, W.P., *Climbing in the British Isles II: Wales and Ireland* (Welsh section), 1896.
Lockington Marshall, W., *The Calf of Man*, 1978.
Moore, A.W. (ed.), *The Manx Notebook*, 1885-7.
Quine, Revd John, Mate's *Isle of Man Illustrated*, 1902.
Radcliffe, Constance, *Shining by the Sea*, 1986.

Designed by Lily Publications Ltd, PO Box 33, Ramsey, Isle of Man, IM99 4LP for The Manx Heritage Foundation.